MOVING THE PIANO

ALSO BY FAITH SHEARIN

The Owl Question
The Empty House

MOVING THE PIANO

FAITH SHEARIN

Stephen F. Austin State University Press
2011

Copyright © Stephen F. Austin State University
All rights reserved.

Stephen F. Austin State University Press
P.O. Box 13007, SFA Station
Nacogdoches, TX   75962-3007
sfapress@sfasu.edu
936.468.1078

Manufactured in the United States of America

LIBRARY OF CONGRESS IN PUBLICATION DATA
Shearin, Faith
Moving the Piano / Faith Shearin
Book Design: Laura McKinney
p. cm.
ISBN: 978-1-936205-40-0

1. Poetry. 2. American Poetry. 3. Shearin, Faith.

The paper used in this book meets the requirements of ANSI/NISO Z39.48-1992
(R1997) (Permanence of Paper)

For my sister Dana and my brother Will
And for Kitty Hawk

ACKNOWLEDGMENTS

Thanks to the editors of the following journals where these poems first appeared:

"Shade" and "Three Dog Night" *Saranac Review,* "Spring Is Dangerous" *Seneca Review,* "Sunburns", "Solo", "The Dead Are Lucky", and "Storage" *North American Review,* "How To Live Without Money" *Salamander,* "The Day After Valentine's" and "Alligators" *Southern Humanities Review,* "The Trouble With Seafood", "Birds and Bees", and "Why I Love A Carousel" *Atlanta Review,* "The Old Boyfriends", "Not Knowing", and "Being Called Ma'am" *Ploughshares,* "The Old Movie Theatre", "Why I Love Swimming Pools", "Beyond Our Means" and "Moving The Piano" *Poetry East,* "Picking the Kitten" *Alaska Quarterly Review.*

This manuscript was written with the help of a grant from the National Endowment for the Arts. Thanks to my parents and grandparents, my siblings, my husband Tom, my daughter Mavis, my friend Bonnie Croskey, and to my Friday writing group: Raymond Atkins, Melanie Sumner, and Adrienne Su. Thanks to the Peaked Hill Trust and the Provincetown Commuinty Compact for two artist residencies in their dune shacks and to the Montana Artists Refuge where some of these poems were written.

Thanks to Jack Driscoll and Michael Delp for years of instruction and encouragement.

CONTENTS

"And because you do not eat
that which rips your heart with joy."

Thomas Lux, "Refrigerator, 1957"

How To Live Without Money

The dead are good at this. Having lost their bodies
they can live anywhere: in a field,

in a closet, in a vase like a flower. Without mouths
there is no need for dishes. Without eyes

there is no need for books. If you practice,
you can imagine you are not hungry; even a child

can make a sandwich out of air. Try riding
through town on a lawn chair pulled by balloons.

Pretend, like the emperor, that you love your new clothes.

Not Knowing

It is the not knowing that keeps us going,
the way we turn the pages of a book.

We don't know which October will bring
hurricanes and which will bring

the bright Conchs that hold open
our doors. We don't know whether

the Blue Heron is pensive
on his big stick legs or if

he has seen a fish. We don't know
whether the sea turtle's eggs will hatch

and, if they do, how many will find
the tide's tongue. We don't know

if the sick dog will get better, if
the argument continues or resolves.

We don't know which year the whales
will pass so close we could touch

their slick backs with our hands.
We try not to know that the story

is short: what matters now will vanish
like snow. We wonder if a friend

will visit, if a gift will arrive, if our children
will come home dusted in happiness.

Our island is disappearing: each year
another row of cottages erased by wind.

Still, we wonder which bright box will hold
onto the sand, which castle will last until noon.

Sunburns

There was the one I got on the lawn of a boarding school in Boston,
bent over my school books, half shielded by the night of a tree.
This was a spring burn: accidental, one arm, my neck. Another on

my roof in New York where I liked to sit after class, drinking tea
with twenty pigeons. Several on purpose in the fields of my college
with a boy who carried wine in his backpack. He liked

the way my face freckled in the light. Once in Utah, hiking
for days without a hat. On Martha's Vineyard on a nude beach
where we covered ourselves in clay. The burns were wonderful:

a way to wear the sun after dark. I loved my warm skin
against a shirt or sheet. Peeling, I pretended I was a snake
who has grown large and must remove what is old, so she can be free.

Moving the Piano

I have seen this in the city on my way
to the dull office of my life: a piano

with a coat, roped and hanging
out a window from some enormous

pulley on the roof. There is the moment
when the bundled elegance swings

clear of the window and shifts
meaningfully in the air. This is before

its descent, before it rests on the sidewalk
like a fallen angel. A piano is meant

to fill a living room: its dark wood
and toothy music a sign of prosperity.

It is not made to dangle from apartment
windows, to twirl above pedestrians

like a hippo on a wire. We cannot
turn away from its startling

moment of freedom, its perilous fling
before it returns to the burdens of this earth.

The Old Movie Theatre

The movie theatre at the end of our street
won't last much longer.
You can tell by the way the seats
have broken and the carpet,
once red, is now pink. You can tell
by the depressed velvet

couch in the ladies' lounge
where my daughter and I sit
when the movie grows sad or violent.
You can see it in the old woman
behind the glass ticket booth,
her hair too white for this world,

her shirt made of fabric and dust.
Each box of popcorn tastes
like the sky before we were born.
Two dogs in the lobby wear
antlers at Christmas and horns
on Halloween and, if we touch

their heads, they sigh. A teenage boy
has been lifting letters
onto a marquee all morning, reaching
into a box of unformed
words, straining to name a movie
and a date. We will have moved

away before the owner can't pay the rent
and the city considers
whether or not to knock it down. But we know
already that the babies across the street
won't grow up playing in the aisles.

We have to find some way to love it
while knowing it's nearly over: our broken
seats wobbly but kind in the plush darkness.
We must love it and say goodbye
to it at once which hurts

the way happiness hurts:
the big, glittering screen,
the soft, faded curtains, the pretty movie
stars flickering like candles.

Spring is Dangerous

Spring is dangerous: no one tells you that.
They talk about birth: the golden chicks

breaking open their eggs, the blooming forest,
Jesus awake in his grave. But this is the season

when sap runs in the trees like blood, the time
of heart attacks and allergies and violent rashes.

This is when the viruses strike: Slap Cheek
or Roseola, strep throat like a red flower.

And the snakes appear, sunning themselves
in the tall grass, their diamonds bright.

This is when my grandparents died, as if
rebirth made them tired, the season when

our first child decided to stop making himself,
his heart like a handkerchief. You can't remake

the world without certain casualties: turtle eggs
in the mouths of foxes, baby squirrels

fallen from trees. People forget how death
is born with each litter, its breath as hot as the sun.

Spelling Bee

In the spelling bee my daughter wore a good
brown dress and kept her hands folded.
There were twelve children speaking

into a microphone that was taller than
they were. Each time it was her turn
I could barely look. It wasn't that I wanted

her to win but I hoped she would be
happy with herself. The words were too hard
for me; I would have missed chemical,

thermos, and dessert. Each time she spelled
one correctly my heart became a bird.
She once fluttered so restlessly beneath

my skin and, on the morning of her arrival,
her little red hands held nothing.
Her life since has been a surprise: she can

sew; she can draw; she can read. She hates
raisins but loves science. All the parents
must feel this, watching from the cheap

folding chairs. Somewhere inside them
love took shape and now
it stands at the microphone, spelling.

The Boat

My husband longs to own a boat.
He dreams of water dark as sleep.
I know he'll leave this earth and float.

He wears desire: that human coat.
All oceans move beneath his feet.
My husband longs to own a boat.

His love for me? A folded note.
Birds and brooms are made to sweep.
I know he'll leave this earth and float.

His compass is a kind of hope.
Hearts and tides are made to beat.
My husband longs to own a boat.

Leaving tugs an anchored rope.
Wind moves the clouds and then the trees.
I know he'll leave this earth and float.

The life he digs is not a moat.
A hull must glide: it has no feet.
My husband longs to own a boat.
I know he'll leave this poem and float.

The Dream

The dream that repeated many times
when I was twenty was a dream
in which I was killing women. Night after

night I went in search of them: women
of all ages and professions, their hair
as sweet as honey, their lips red

and swollen like fruit. I had a lake
where I waited for them to appear
and they came to me out of the forest:

their faces without expression,
their feet bare; they came the way
an animal might come to its owner.

I wrapped them in silk, as if I was
a spider, and they let me do this
for they were sleepwalking in my psyche:

women without their own intentions,
dumb mummies. I covered them up,
pushed them into the lake, where

they floated for a moment like white boats
without direction. Then the water
swallowed them, night after night,

the lake's surface calm despite the struggle
below. No one lived. I woke in a sweat
of guilt: my boyfriend's arm around

my ribs, the moon's mood in my window.
I was trying to decide who I would be,
what costume I would wear to work,

what man I would love. And at night
I was killing women, all the women
I could not become, and sometimes

they touched me with their cold hands,
and sometimes the weight of them
was too much and I lost my balance,
for a moment, at the water's edge.

The Trouble with Seafood

It comes wrapped in shells and scales and full
of tiny bones that choke. I grew up by the sea

so I should like the smell of fish markets,
know how to crack a crab leg or open

an oyster. I should like shrimp cocktail:
pink ovaries, red sauce. The trouble

is that the ocean is feminine and the moon
makes her swell. Each creature pulled

from her salt smells like blood. Even in
restaurants where patrons are expensive

and pressed and leaned over white tablecloths,
the seafood is obscene. And impossible to eat:

all that prying and digging for the smallest
piece of meat. I never liked being a woman

and I am disturbed by my body of water.
I can be opened; I have a second mouth.

And I hate blood: its smells and stains.
Tourists wear bibs when they eat lobster:

that great cockroach boiled and served
with lemon. When I watch them tear it open,

hear the crack of the shell, I cross my arms, my legs.

Swearing

My father loved to swear: each word
like a bird uncaged. He was going to
sue the bastards. A household appliance
he could not repair was a goddamned
motherfucker. He feared being piss poor.
He drove us to school, muttering under
his breath, each office hassle named
Jesus H. Christ. My mother worried
we'd pick it up. Sometimes she said
his name, Norman, and reminded him
that we could hear. We loved his swearing:
each delightful forbidden word which
lit a room like fire. When he went into
the yard to fix a fence he spoke to every
impossible detail, loud enough for the
neighbors to hear. The boards were
pieces of shit and the shovel was busted.
All day, repairing the fence, he was
going to fuck the fucking fuckers.
My teachers, grandparents, and friends
lived in places where words were cleaner:
gosh darn, oops, and oh my like folded
laundry. My father spoke in chocolate,
whatever he felt filled the house like a pie.

Keeping Cool

All the long summers of my North Carolina childhood
I was hot. In the back of my grandmother's car
where the air conditioning did not blow, in the cabin

by the river where we swam and wore our wet
bathing suits to bed. At the store where we walked
for popsicles which dyed our mouths orange. On porches

in rocking chairs with glasses of tea. One cousin
taught me to hold ice cubes to my wrist, another liked
washcloths hung over the face of a fan. It was hot

and the dogs were still at our feet and the cats slept
under the bed. We didn't cook in the kitchen, we ate
tomato sandwiches. We didn't turn on the lights,

we ruined our eyes trying to read. In the afternoons
great thunder clouds gathered and lightning struck
our chimneys and trees. Heat was like the men

who had jobs they hated and babies who cried
and mortgages they could not pay. It was like
housewives cutting sandwiches in the shape of stars.

It was like me in my thin sexless body listening
to rock and roll songs about love. The thunderstorms
were an argument – slapped cheeks, slammed doors –

and afterwards, for a little while, the air was cool and clear.

Alligators

The year she is six my daughter dreams
of alligators in the closet: at home where
her uniform waits and at school
where the children hang their coats
in a room made of winter. When certain
classmates begin stealing her lunch
she imagines an alligator passing behind
her teacher's desk, unnoticed. Sometimes
the alligator is on our street, eating cars.
Sometimes it wanders to the playground
where she is hopping from one square
to another, practicing balance. I don't
like sending her into the dull weather
of the classroom: blackboard like
a starless sky. Alligators in the fountain
where she stoops to drink her water.
Alligators in the desks with freshly
sharpened pencils. Alligators leading
the children through the unlit hallways,
tails swishing like skirts.

Picking the Kitten

You had to hold it awhile in your hand.
It was important to look into the box

of blind fur and notice who needed you.
Not the one who chased its tail,

not the one who slept in a corner
with an air of indifference. There were

colors and markings to consider.
Which would you want to find

on your pillow? The one I took home
was warm as fever. I held her purr

in my pocket, her roughness on my
bedroom rug. I pour out this memory

the way I poured out her evening cream.

The Old Boyfriends

They return in my father's ghostly sailboat,
never steady, and in spring when my body

is like a maple tree. Their purpose is to imagine
the life we did not choose. One lives in a house

with a cat, mountains in the distance. Their job
is to tend my younger self: that other body.

One is hiking by day, carving cabinets at night.
They are just as I left them or they left me.

They are in my daughter's questions,
in the towns where I was young. I left one

in a restaurant after the food was ordered
so he dined alone with two burritos, two iced teas.

Killing Butterflies

Find a net, a moment in the yard when
you see beauty unfolding like a pair

of wings. The butterfly is hope: ugly mortal
self wrapped like a mummy and risen again.

Angels are not as stunning as a painted lady
or a red admiral. This is why, long ago,

people trapped them in Stifling Boxes:
containers thrown into boiling water.

And why, before that, collectors asphyxiated
them with the flames of sulphur matches.

It is terrible and human to capture butterflies,
to pin them in a box so we can look at

them whenever we like. It is harder to know
they are leaving even as we have just

seen them in the garden, glowing like jewels.

The Day after Valentine's

Love is cheaper now: fifty cent stuffed animals,
deflated balloons that declare *I love you*

but not that much. Chocolates melting
in their thin plastic hearts. Holidays are

arbitrary pressure, aisles of red light.
I am sad the day after anything

but expired love is worse than
old Halloween or faded Easter. The bins

of passed over kittens and hollow
chocolate flowers like stubs from a movie

I saw with a boy who forgot my name.
The one who told jokes that weren't funny,

the one who was handsome but dumb. All that
old love on sale: less valuable but never free.

Storage

That year we left the house we couldn't afford and put
our belongings in storage. We were free now
to travel or live in tiny spaces. We kept our chairs

and tables in a cement cell, our bookshelves,
our daughter's old toys, clothes we wouldn't wear
or discard. There were books we liked but did not

need and mattresses and pots and pans. Sometimes
we went to visit our things: sat in our rocking chairs,
searched for a jacket, listened to an old radio. It was like

visiting someone I loved in a hospital: the way, removed
from the world, a person or object becomes thin,
diminished. The furniture on which we lived

our young life had no job but to wait for us.
It remembered our dinners, the light through
our windows, the way the baby once played on the floor.

What the Children Do

They grow up, I tell you, though this is no brilliant revelation.
It is slow at first then all at once like mushrooms in rain.
The baby has no words then one hundred words

then enough words to tell a joke. They begin as an idea,
a longing, a lack of caution. Then they are climbing
the staircase, waving their arms like trees. You lift them

from sleep and they settle their head between your
breast and chin. Then you step into their room again
and they are as long as the bed and they are telling you

the story of their dreams. When my daughter was a toddler
we spent each winter at the mall where we met old women
wrapped in memory, eager to hold her tight. *They grow up*

so quickly they said and I rushed to take her out of their
arms which were thin and brittle and speckled like death.

Being Called Ma'am

The summer I turn forty I pretend I am still young enough
to sit with my college self at the library before disappearing

in a field of smoke. Don't my jeans still fit? Can't I see
without glasses if I just hold the book a little farther

from my face? Then, hiking with my daughter, I find
myself talking to a group of college boys, the sort

I would have gone camping with twenty years before,
their faces like unused maps. And when they answer

they call me ma'am, that word their mothers taught them,
or some old schoolmarm maybe, demanding respect.

A distance opens between the woman they see and the one
of my imagination and I am not someone they might laugh with

in the library but instead the stern face that appears from
behind the stacks to remind them of their manners.

I am the finger over the lips: sexless, as heavy as silence.

Why I Love Swimming Pools

I grew up in a resort town where they were
as frequent as houses. I love their false blue

which is more vivid than the sky and their shapes:
rectangle, L, oval, diamond. Some have waterfalls,

palm trees that rustle just above your head.
I like the smell of chlorine, the ladies

in sunglasses as still as human sacrifices
on their chaise lounges. There are umbrellas,

those swirls of happiness, and lifeguards dressed
in eternal youth. We wear sunscreen

thick with coconut oil and the rooms where we change
into swimsuits are like the telephone booths

Superman used. Like him we are different in our new form:
weightless, able to jump from high places and survive.

Solo

It's easier than I think. The bed holds the shape
of a valley and the space beside me

is a hill. Or, on the front porch in morning,
I am touched by objects: tea glass,

straw chair, light filtered by the fingers
of a tree. My shirt has the weight of a kiss.

Nuns and monks live this way: robes,
habits, their minds full of wine and prayer.

My hands have been licked by wild dogs.
I have been loved by cities: warm cab rides

to darkened theatres, museums with rooms
of nudes. Sunbathing, I have been remade

by tongues of light. In this cottage, ocean
in my window, wind like a tea kettle,

I am a lovely cup.

The Meaning of Clean

I have been looking for the meaning of clean.
Money is dirty but wealthy people are clean.
Women are dirty but men are clean.

Door handles are never clean because
they have been touched a million times
by hands. Virgins and nuns are clean.

Mountain air is clean. Babies are clean.
Clean people are better than dirty people.
Clean things sparkle; they are spotless,

unsullied, unstained. Untidy people are lazy.
If you clean a tub or an oven you must
get down on your hands and knees

as if you are praying. Love is clean
but desire is dirty. Surgery requires
a sterile field. If you have not been arrested

your record is clean. Stars are clean
and night is clean and cold. Swearing
is dirty and flies are dirty and mice

are so dirty they brought plagues
on their backs. In a neighborhood
the tidy have the right to dislike the untidy.

Dust gathers like disapproval. If you
have quit a drink or a drug you are clean.
Sin is unclean but baptism is cleansing.

Your parents may ask you to clean your room.
Janitors and maids make very little money
because anyone can clean but nobody

wants to. Most houses are cleaned
by women though they themselves
are unclean. If you don't wash

your hands you may catch an infection.

Memory

There is a street in childhood you may remember,
a woman who used to fold laundry while you sat
on a red carpet surrounded by trees. Your mother

was getting ready for a dinner party: her hair
piled high on her head, her dress so long it might
belong to a bride. If you turn left you will find

your father behind his first desk and if you turn
right your mother has taken your hand and is
skipping with you down a sidewalk towards

a diner with a long bar where they serve doughnuts
as sweet as sleep. No wind blows here, no
umbrellas open or close. If you travel further south

your grandparents are still young and you have
spent the night in their bed where part of your
story begins. There is a train you might take,

each seat wide and soft. And a car your daughter
has never seen where your suitcase waits
in a trunk full of love and soup. I don't know how

to get there anymore though sometimes a smell
or flavor opens the floor beneath my feet.
Certain forest shadows have pointed the way.

I have found the old roads in closet boxes,
addresses in books that smell of autumn,
the past like a pile of color: each leaf a hand.

Farmers

They know what weather decides.
As a child my grandfather dressed himself

by the fire of dawn. He wore a hat
but his face was always turned up,

watching the sky. Clouds and insects
were the plot, life or death determined

by the timing of a frost. His father
taught him: no two plants or animals

are alike. They stood together
in houses of smoke where tobacco

hung over them like pleasure. In those
deep summer fields their hunger grew tall.

Tired

There is the kind of tired when you have been walking
for miles along a beach, or swimming for hours,
where you need to sit down and drink,

very slowly, a glass of night. Then there is the fatigue
caused by worry, by standing at a window waiting
for a ship to come home, the wind weeping

at the front door, the sails just beyond the horizon.
Or the sort of tired that comes after a party:
the result of conversations, cheerful insults, food

spilled across your chest like embarrassment.
I have been sick and tired: a fever in my blood's ocean,
my pillow like a raft. I have been tired of a person:

the things they will likely say, their mood
like a weather I endure. There is the exhaustion
that comes after an argument you cannot quite

resolve, the insults like thorns in your shoes.
Then there is travel: the dust in your plans,
the struggle of luggage, great swaying of the train.

There is the aftermath of nights when sleep
was a package that would not arrive. Was I
ever rested? After awhile you are always tired,

always looking for a better bed, a place
to rest your eyes, a nice chair, a vacation.

Mailbox

All that summer I could not get warm. I had a new playhouse:
big as a bedroom, perfectly square, with glass windows
I could open or close. This was the June I got sick: high fever,
pain in my side, nausea so deep all food tasted rotten.
I kept a candle in there, a box of damp matches, a blanket,
my books which smelled like fur. I swept the floor
until it was bare, imagined building a table
I could fold into a bed; I looked over the hot green fingers
of the lawn. My father made a garden of giant squash
and watermelons as big as my baby sister. It was
the fertilizer, he said, when the neighbors came by to comment
or admire. Sometimes he sent them home with a bag of earth.
I was so sick I wore my nightgown like a dress and while
doctors studied my throat my sister was cradled
in the arms of nurses who admired her eyelashes, her perfect
clamshell hands. What were they looking for?
I was embarrassed by the way they undressed me.
Sometimes they made me pee in a cup but first a nurse
told me how to clean myself: front to back. They didn't
want my early dirty urine but what came later. I only
had a few years before blood and breasts, before my body
became like the playhouse with the garden out front.
It was August when they found the kidney infection.
Kidneys, they said, did the cleaning so I could see
I wasn't as tidy as everyone else. But I wanted to be.
Not much time before I outgrew my house, before
it was my sister's turn to step inside. At first my head
hit the door frame if I didn't bend down. Then I built
a mailbox which stood empty, my name on the side.

Three Dog Night

In the old days, before houses were warm,
people did not sleep alone. Not even
widows went by themselves into

the cold sheets of night. Rooms were
lit with lanterns and children were
encouraged to jump on their beds,

warming themselves, before they
crawled inside. You might sleep with
your cousin or sister, your nose

buried in the summer of their
hair. You might place a baked potato
in your blanket to help it remember

warmth. A fire would be lit but, after
awhile, it would smolder down
to the bone silence of ash. Everything

was cold: the basin where you washed
your face, the wood floor, the windows
where you watched your breath

open over the framed blur of snow.
Your hands and feet were cold
and the trees were cold: naked,

traced in ice. You might take a dog
to bed or two or three, anything to lie
down with life, feel it breathing nearby.

Beyond our Means

This is the phrase you use to describe what we
cannot have. You learned it in childhood,
peering into the windows of all you did

not own. When you say it I picture a blonde couple
on a yacht wearing mink coats, several houses tended
by maids, a decorative leopard pacing in the yard.

Beyond our means: vacations, laughter, flowers.
We cannot own the world because we are
too poor. Sunlight does not bend for us;

music is a river in another village. We cannot
own sleep; wild foxes live in a den we
will never glimpse. Balloons and clouds float

just out of reach. Beside me in our bed you
have grown as faint as the stars in a city sky.
We are defined by what we don't have, what is

not possible, all the places we will not see.
On our ancient nautical map we slip between
dragons: the edge of what is ours as flat as

any theory that pretends to know the earth's shape.

Insomnia

As if I've forgotten the syllables of my own name.
I can go to sleep: down the stairs,

into a corridor of darkness, but I cannot stay.
I remember how easy it was when

I was young, how my eyes closed
and I found myself in a moon canoe,

paddling through a lake of stars.
I did not worry whether or not

it would happen; I did not find myself
suddenly alert and unable to return.

I am so helpless now with my mugs
of frustration, my flock of problems.

I am always buying something
for the bed as though the answer

is inside my pillow. I think of the old
men I found on couches all through

my childhood, napping loudly,
or my grandmothers rattling in the

night kitchen. I think of Rip Van Winkle
who spent twenty years in the land

I half remember. How did he find that
patch of grass? Did he use his beard
as a blanket?

The Dead Are Lucky

They don't have annual pap smears and mammograms.
They don't spend several days a week in the maze
of the supermarket where food rises in great walls,

each jar like an eye. They are not expected at family
gatherings where no one likes them. They don't have
a job they hate or a body that has fattened with age.

They don't own anything so they don't waste time
maintaining it: trimming the grass, washing the car.
I'm not saying their lives are ideal – they miss sex,

for instance, and the flavor of peaches in summer.
They miss the weight and warmth of the baby
in their arms. They miss beer and love letters

and clean sheets. But their lives have ended: they can't
make any new mistakes. Gossip has blown away
like ash. Sometimes I envy the shadows where

they disappear, the graveyards where they gather
to laugh. I envy the way they can love one another
without jealousy, outside the tiny coffin of time.

The Right Angle

It was hard for the photographer to take
a good picture of me. He had to stand

on a ladder, umbrellas of light around
my head. I am forty now so my face

is wide and used and my neck might
belong to a rooster; I have blood vessels

that make shapes like constellations
in the night sky. This man began to sweat,

peering down at me through his lens,
trying to find the right angle. He was

hoping to emphasize some things
and not others. Who could blame him?

The world prefers younger women. He did
eventually take something flattering

but I knew the beauty in it was conjured.
It wasn't me the way the waitress

at my favorite diner sees me
or the way my daughter sees me,

in my old pajamas, bringing her breakfast
down the hall so she can sleep an extra

fifteen minutes, her gratitude like beauty.

Drawing Pictures

We are leaned over the sand, drawing pictures
of places we have been. I sketch an apartment
above an Italian restaurant. You never saw

me sleeping there: my window open,
night pouring into my kitchen. There were mice
in my cupboards with feet as soft as kisses.

You never soaked in the old bathtub with feet,
its water as warm as tears. We never walked
together on my roof which had craters

like the moon. You drew a mountain where
you counted money in a vault; you drew
a ski lift because you had to go up

to come down. Now we are getting closer
to the place where you returned to me,
dressed in summer's skin, my building's

elegance made of some other era. I am drawing
now the house where we lived after
we were married. They have knocked it down

so only we can reconstruct it. Remember
the closet where our clothes practiced
hanging together in darkness? My dress

considered your pants. Now, the attic where
we watched the rain gather. I don't know
how we opened the door in the floor

or how we carried our boxes up those
thin stairs. Always, before we draw
something new, we erase what came

first with the flat of our hands.

Cats

I had cats before we were married: feral ones,
spotted ones, one with no tail from a box
in a dusty summer street. If I saw a cat

I was likely to feed it and you know
how tribes of them followed me through
the dunes, their tails held high.

I still want one though I know I cannot
have it. I miss their balance, their whiskers
which are full of feeling. Cats don't want

to be walked; they don't offer kindness
with their tongues. They did not need me,
really, though certain strays entered my bed:

dug their claws into my shoulder, a jungle
of love in their throats. I liked the wild ones
who did not live with me but came to

my door sometimes, their pupils like black flames.

Terra

I grew up watching *Gone With the Wind*
with my grandmothers, rehearsing

for my life as Scarlett or Melanie. On the bright
steps of my southern childhood I practiced

pinching my cheeks, holding my breath
while someone else tied my corsets.

I could make a dress out of curtains.
I could deliver a baby while, outside,

Atlanta burned. When the wagon took me
home to Terra I would save the plantation

by murder or marriage, my hat tied
beneath my chin in a cheerful bow.

Like Melanie I would forgive anything,
befriend prostitutes, donate my wedding ring

to the soldiers. Someone would kiss me
in a field where cotton no longer bloomed.

I would want whatever I could not have.
I would die trying to have another child.

My husband would never recover from
loving me: my shape on that marble staircase,

too restless for an afternoon nap.

Christmas Trees

We were usually too late to buy a regular tree.
I can count on one hand the years when my parents
found one on time and adorned it with angels

or lights. Other times we improvised.
My mother favored branches hauled in
from the yard and covered in origami birds.

Once we arrived on the tree lot so late
there was only one sickly contender, no longer
standing, its needles falling like rain. My sister

covered this one with so much white tinsel
it looked hairy: a silent Cousin Itt.
One year we left our tree sleeping

in the corner, brushed away the needles,
its shape slender and skeletal by spring. We did not
take it down. The next year we wrapped it

in candy canes and popcorn balls, the branches
surprised by their good fortune.
Our neighbors had fresh, elegant trees and rooftops

outlined in lights. They had plastic Santas
and poinsettias with violent red petals.
Their Christmas cards arrived in our mailbox:

families dressed in matching shirts, smiling
at us from sunny beaches. It is, afterall, a season
of appearances disguised as giving: fruit cakes

delivered in festive tins. Our trees were late
and strange but we did not give up trying to have
them, not for many years: the corner of our

living room continuously surprised by
our humor, our courage, our willingness
to decorate whatever we might find.

Mission Control

I was watching a film about space missions in 1969
and I saw the handsome, brave men preparing

to be shot through the stars. These astronauts said
they accepted risk and I saw them wearing

the white suits which might prevent burning
or freezing: fish bowls around their heads,

hoses behind them like tails. They wanted to go
where no man had gone before: into the darkness

above the suburban houses where they first began
to dream. Wives and mothers waited on the ground,

in Texas, gravity in their faces. They were not yet
allowed to orbit; they did not collect moon rocks

or plant flags. The moon hung over our country
like a newly exposed breast. Even now

I am counting the places where I have been
excluded: an explosion beneath me, darkness

expanding inside me like space.

The Fox

It was an ordinary morning: November, thin light,
and we paused over our pancakes to watch
something red move outside. Our house is on

an untamed patch of land and, across the lagoon,
another house surrounded by trees. On the banks
of their shore, facing us: a fox. We thought

he might be a dog at first for he trotted and sniffed
like a dog but when he turned to us
we knew he was nobody's pet. His face was arranged

like a child's face – playful, dainty – and his eyes
were liquid and wild. He stood for awhile, looking out,
as if he could see us in our pajamas, then found

a patch of sand beneath a tree and turned himself
into a circle of fur: his head tucked into his tail.
It was awful to watch him sleep: exposed,

tiny, his eyes closed. How can any animal
be safe enough to rest? But while I washed
our dishes he woke again, yawned, and ran

away to the places only foxes know. My God
I was tired of being a person. Even now his tail
gestures to me across the disapproving lagoon.

Jellyfish

They drifted in oceans before
dinosaurs and move as I do –

urged by currents, unsure of
their own pulse. In pictures their tentacles

hang like hair beneath the hat
of their domes. They might be kites

released in a wet sky; like fetuses
they unfurl in salt. On beaches

they suggest sex: ovaries, penises.
There is anger in their touch,

venom released without teeth.
Here come the ocean's brides: headless

veils awaiting some troubled union.

Adam Naming the Animals

After he could no longer speak with them,
after the warm garden had a draft,

and Adam found himself naked and mortal,
after his wife was made from his own

cage of love, and after she introduced
him to the snake that offered its famous

advice, after all these things, God asked
Adam to name the animals. Eve would

bring forth children in great pain
but Adam must name the beasts,

one by one, remembering how he had
known them, how they once had voices

as clear as the difference between
good and evil. He felt the loss of their

friendship: he used to rely on the birds
to watch the future and the dogs to sniff

the past. Now he had names for them
but they had no name for him,

their thoughts as hidden as the wishes
of trees. God spoke loudly

and set things on fire but the animals
were now as silent as snow, traveling

on their many legs, wrapped in fur
or feathers. Adam was lonely and less able

to see the world, though the fruit he'd eaten
promised clarity. Naming the animals

was hard because it was like naming
all the parts of himself he no longer

knew, all the parts he could not understand.

Where the Birds Go

Birds travel between heaven and earth: they have wings
like angels and bones made to float. This is why

they gather on beaches to discuss the meaning of life.
It is why I stare into the trees at the bright promise

of their songs. You may have noticed how far
the owl can see into the past, how the parrot

can speak. A crow once followed me for a decade,
its head tilted as if it could hear the other world.

You know how it feels to have a bird in the house:
how suddenly it is trapped, like us. I knew a man who lost

all his children in a car accident. He began to look
for birds: made a life list, traveled to far away places

to catch a glimpse of a certain kind of beak or plumage.
Of course, he was looking for his children in the only

trees he could reach; he knew where the birds go.

Summer Hotels

That summer we lived in hotels. Some waited
by the sea and had the wide hallways
and big swimming pools of another era.
There were ballrooms where no one danced,

smoking lounges where the air was still.
In cities we lived among business people
who drank coffee in elevators, around
them a smell of hurry and cologne. My husband

went to work but my daughter and I stayed
behind: learned the contents of linen closets,
listened to maids talking in the hall where
they pushed great carts of soap and boredom.

We watched wedding parties drunk on cake,
groups of people meeting in stale rooms,
their names taped to their hearts. We liked
the big beds, the way we were erased

each day: hotel like a beach, staff
like a tide. We watched so many things
from our balcony where we perched
like migrating birds, our feathers wild.

Winter

There is some child on the playground who likes
to hurt my daughter. I have never seen her though

I imagine her white teeth. She is just a child yet
her presence has brought winter, my daughter

cold in her coat. The insults she has hurled
are frozen like breath in the air. Children have not

learned to hide what they feel so the weather
inside them is also outside: deep as snow.

No matter how I dress my daughter the wind
finds her skin. No matter how I love her there

will be no warmth she can wear through
fourth grade. There will be winter again and again:

her skin raw, her fingers stiff in their mittens.

Jealousy

Here is what caused
Snow White's stepmother
to dress as a witch
and poison an apple,
why Cinderella needed magic
to attend her first ball. It was
the tower around Rapunzel,
the forest that darkened
over Hansel and Gretel,
the cause of the curse that pricked
Sleeping Beauty's future, what
the wolf felt when he saw
the basket of food packed for
some beloved grandmother.
When I was nine my parents
decided to have another child.
Each white gift that arrived
was not for me and the room
they painted was a place
where I would not sleep.
I wanted to be the person they
were waiting for, the one
they were hoping to hold.
I imagined being wrapped
in excitement, my crib
lit with pillows and milk.
Every way I posed for love
was too large, too familiar.
My face was made of germs.

What Merlin Knew

Merlin knew the whole story before it happened:
how Arthur would love Guinevere,
why that love would ruin him. He knew

each knight who would sit at the round table,
the chairs named before some of them
were born. Also the magic that would

cause Lancelot to marry Elaine,
her body destined to float
by candlelight on a boat made of grief.

The sons of Arthur and Lancelot would
be born of lies, not love, to women
they did not mean to embrace. For awhile

Merlin lived in the castle with his books
and herbs but he could not stand to watch.
Instead he followed the Lady of the Lake

to her house of tides. It is her hand we see
when Arthur is dying, saving the sword.
Anyway, knowing is like living under water:

quiet and heavy, all light filtered
through the tail of a fish.

Ordinary Medicine

I don't want an ordinary medicine.
Not a bandage for my hand or a bottle
for my grief. I want my father dressed
in youth, his kite as light as sky.
Send back this torn paper lantern.
Send back the doctor whose questions
are an eye. I want my childhood by the sea,
my grandmother's hair undone so it falls
like night. I want my cat again, twenty
years dead but still licking her dinner.
I want what was taken from me by breathing.

The Bell

If a leper needed to leave the colony
he or she would ring a bell
or wear one around their neck

like a cow. Anyone who feared
infection scattered at the sound:
roads opened, store lines grew short.

Lepers were given a different sort
of money so their germs would not
disappear into a pocket. What lepers

carried was ugliness and this is feared
like death. All day the young ones run,
chasing beauty, and the older ones

just behind them, determined
to keep up. Ugliness belongs
on an island, surrounded by storms,

for if it comes among us we might
not hear it. We might touch it
without knowing, fill our hands

with its whisper, find it sleeping
inside us like an animal.

Yellow Fever

It began with the rains in Africa.
Winter, the wet season,

mosquitoes hatched and the monkeys
were the first to take ill: their silence

deep in the canopy of trees.
Ships off the coast would carry

ivory, salt and copper laced
with poison eggs to my

southern cousins: ancestors wading
the waterlogged streets of a hot

January, when the hyacinths,
confused, practiced their early blooms.

Birds and Bees

When my daughter starts asking I realize
I don't know which, if any, birds
have penises. I can't picture how swans

do it. I'm even confused about bees:
that fat queen and her neurotic workers,
her children grown in cells. I'm worried

by turtles and snakes: their parts hidden
in places I have never seen. How do they
undress? Long ago, awash in college

boyfriends, I knew a little about sex.
I understood the dances and calls,
the pretty plumage. Now, I am as ignorant

as a child. We have gone to the library
to find books though I know sex
is too wild for words. The desire to be

kissed is the desire to live forever
in the mouth of pleasure. My God
I can never tell my daughter the truth.

It is a secret the way spring is a secret,
buried in February's fields. It is a secret
the way babies are a secret: hidden

by skin or egg, their bodies made of darkness.

Geese

A gaggle of geese return to our street each winter
while migrating from one place to another.
They arrive in January, around my husband's birthday,

and I am surprised to find them behind our house,
honking like cab drivers in traffic. Most leave with
babies but one pair can't manage to have any;

I've watched them sit for years on a wet nest of death,
warming unhappiness. It is only when the other
geese swim past them, proudly displaying

a line of live chicks, that they realize they have
failed again, their eggs silent beneath the love
of their feathers. My neighbors and I don't agree

on much but we all watch these geese from our
windows, with binoculars sometimes, our breakfast
growing cold on the table. We wish the unsuccessful

ones would have a season of luck, their eggs healthy
and well placed, for each of us has known the pleasure
of spring, the way it feels for something closed

to open: the soft, heavenly weather of arrival.

Dead Pets

My brother lists all the pets we killed.
Not on purpose, of course, but because
we were young. He had a parakeet
that died flying into a mirror, its vanity

as lethal as poison. My sister's Iguana
took ill after a draft in winter. Two hamsters,
sold to us as brothers, produced a litter
of pink children: as blind and hairless

as worms. Several cats fell through the ice
of our canal which was thin as a cracker.
We brought these animals we did not
understand to live beside us in rooms

too hot or too cold. Sometimes we won
them as a prize at a party. We had a bag
of food or a bright cage. We meant well
and knew they were living creatures

like ourselves. Still, our house did not
suit them. We liked their wildness:
the distance they traveled to join us,

the unknown places from which they came.
We liked their silence: their fur or feathers,
their tails, their sandpaper tongues.
Our childhoods were marked by their

comings and goings: the cat in the closet
giving birth on my father's best dress shoes.

Big Foot

He is out there somewhere, in the woods
with chipmunks and deer. He looks like us

but taller, wilder, covered in hair. We have found
the print of his feet in mud, his big scat

near streams. He is at least seven feet tall
and seen mostly with his broad back turned,

as if his attention is elsewhere. He might be
our ancestor, unevolved. We seek him

in the caves of myth. He lives where
we once slept, before pavement or skyscrapers.

Chasing him is like looking behind
while running ahead, like measuring a shadow

for clothes. As with all theories
there are believers and non-believers,

scientists and witches. There is the visible world
and the invisible one and he lives somewhere

in between. You cannot touch him
but you can see him run; you cannot find his bones

but you can hear him moving: heavily, in the trees.

Foot Binding

A girl as young as four but no older than six
would be taken into the kitchen. It was

the mother's job to do this and it began
with a soak in warm water, a massage.

A mother shapes her daughter, gives her
the form the world prefers, so you

will have to forgive her for what she does
next: breaking four toes with a hammer,

wrapping the feet so they will not grow.
In other countries and times the mother

tightens a corset (that cage meant to
hold breath), cuts away pleasure

between a daughter's legs with a knife.
It is the mother who must do

such things though the feet ache and rot,
the organs never recover. Mother is

the world's instrument, her love
in the kitchen where she prepares a bowl

of water, calls her daughter's name.

I'd Rather be the Father

Right from the start, it's easier to be the father: no morning
nausea, no stretch marks. You can wait outside the

delivery room and keep your clothes on. Notice how
closely the word *mother* resembles *smother*, notice

how she is either too strict or too lenient: wrong for giving up
everything or not enough. Psychology books blame her

for whatever is the matter with all of us while the father
slips into the next room for a beer. I wanted to be

the rational one, the one who told a joke at dinner.
If I were her father we would throw a ball across

the lawn while the grill fills with smoke. But who
wants to be the mother? Who wants to tell her what

to wear and deliver her to the beauty shop and explain
bras and tampons? Who wants to show her what

a woman still is? I am supposed to teach her how to
wash the dishes and do the laundry only I don't want

her to grow up and be like me. I'd rather be the father
who tells her she is loved; I'd rather take her fishing

and teach her to skip stones across the lake of history;
I'd rather show her how far she can spit.

Our Island is Ruled by Wind

Our island is ruled by wind. I don't mean breezes
in summer: that gentle rustling like the sound
of a baby just waking from an afternoon nap.
This is the wind that blew Mary Poppins onto

Cheery Tree Lane, the wind that stands at the window
like a wolf. Sometimes it sings like a tea kettle;
it surrounds us like water; even the trees
are excited by its force. It lifted the first airplane

on a dune not far from here; it wrecked
so many ships we have maps of their crashes:
a fleet of ghosts. It decides which cottages
will disappear in the ocean's white fury. It can

change the mood in a room, take the thing
you are holding away from you, fill your pockets,
say your name. It carries secrets and smells
like a neighbor who loves to gossip. It moves

the rocking chairs and opens the doors; it blows
my papers all over the room; it drops sand
in our food and carries our kites so high
they disappear. To walk against it you must

bend forward and close your eyes: as if you are
sleepwalking, as if you know the sound of dreams.

Leaving

If you mean to leave you must look straight ahead.
For instance when Rhett Butler leaves

Scarlett O'Hara he is sick of the way
she loves someone else and the door

he slams behind him is made of disappointment.
When I left my child to cry in her crib,

purple with fury, I found I could enjoy
nothing; the sound of her unhappiness

made the day dark and small. I have left
behind years of my life the way you might

leave flowers on a grave. I have left my
daughter at the door of the school, her

backpack filled with dread. I have left
the room, the conversation, the party

and sat instead on the porch with the dogs.
Sleep is like leaving your clothes on the shore

of a river so you can swim. Leaving night
for day means the sky will erupt in blood.

Birth is a way of coming and going at once
which is why everyone in the room must cry.

Biltmore Estate

It's easy to disapprove of opulence: it resembles greed.
Even the Vanderbilts could not afford their Biltmore Estate
but this didn't stop them from building it: four acres

of floor space, turrets and towers, made of Indiana Limestone,
facing east. Here George Washington Vanderbilt dreamed
his own mountain kingdom: a 70,000 gallon indoor pool,

two story library with secret passages, elevators,
43 bathrooms so no one would ever have to share.
To the rear an endless porch and to the north a stable

of strong horses protecting his vision from the wind.
He didn't consider how he would repair it or staff it
or afford its heat; he thought instead of French Renaissance

manors, the vast vacation homes his siblings built
in Newport and Hyde Park. Likewise the Titanic:
built for three years but destroyed in hours. Each first class

parlor suite ticket cost four thousand dollars. It carried
40,000 eggs, 3,000 bags of mail, 75,000 pounds of meat,
an automobile. It was the biggest, the first one

with a pool and if they didn't have enough life boats it was
because they made the deck look crowded. I can't help but
admire the dreams that are too wild and elegant to afford,

the ones that cost seven million dollars and break
in half the first time they are used. George Vanderbilt bought
a ticket to ride the Titanic but had a change of plans,

lucky man. He returned to his manor which did not save him
from dying young but gave him a chance to entertain, a place
to show what wealth could buy, a way to shock

visitors who could not help but feel breathless
when they saw the sheer size of his desire, his perilous want,
the glorious insanity of what he had done.

Turtle in the Road

It was the spring before we moved again, a list of what
we must do on the refrigerator, when my daughter
and I found a turtle in the road. He was not gentle
or shy, not properly afraid of the cars that swerved

around his mistake. I thought I might encourage him
towards safety with a stick but each time I touched
his tail he turned fiercely to show me what he thought
of my prodding. He had a raisin head, the legs of

a fat dwarf, the tail of a dinosaur. His shell was a deep
green secret he had kept his whole life. I could not tell
how old he was but his claws suggested years of
reaching. I was afraid to pick him up, afraid of the way

he snapped his jaws, but I wanted to help him return
to the woods which watched him with an ancient
detachment. I felt I understood him because I didn't
want to move either; I was tired of going from one place

to another: the introductions, the goodbyes. I was sick
of getting ready, of unpacking, of mail sent to places
where I used to live. At last I put my stick away
and left him to decide which direction was best.

If I forced him off the road he might return later.
My daughter and I stood awhile, considering him.
He was a traveler from the time of reptiles, a creature
who wore his house like a jacket. I don't know

if he survived his afternoon in the road; I am still
thinking of the way his eyes watched me go.
I can't forget his terrible legs, so determined
to take him somewhere, his tail which pointed
behind him at the dark spaces between the trees.

Teaching Mavis to Ride a Bike

We practiced in Baltimore's alleys with her dress
tucked in so it would not catch in her wheels.

It was late summer and we waited until after supper
when the sun melts. I held the seat and handlebars

and she pedaled as fast as she could. She has
such thin legs, such balance. It did not take

long before she left me standing in place:
hands in my pockets, throat full of hope.

The Last Swim of Summer

Our pool is still blue but a few leaves
have fallen, floating on the surface

of summer. The other swimmers
went home last week, tossed

their faded bathing suits aside,
so my daughter and I are alone

in the water which has grown colder
like a man's hand at the end of

a romance. The lifeguard is under
her umbrella but her bags are packed

for college. We are swimming against
change, remembering the endless

shores of June: the light like lemonade,
fireflies inside our cupped hands,

watermelon night. We are swimming
towards the darkness of what

is next, walking away from the sounds
of laughter and splashing, towels

wrapped around the dampness of our loss.

Remembering our Duck Pond

I want to go back there and spread our blankets
over the green fields where we were young.

Do you remember the sidewalks we followed,
the way the houses grew larger with each block?

In the beginning I pushed your stroller
but later you rode your bike. Sometimes we had

friends with us and our pockets were full
of crackers for the ducks. There was a climbing

tree that rose like a ladder to the sky, a stream
that still remembers your child feet. There were

fish with brilliant orange tails just below
the pond's surface. I read books aloud while

you drew pictures of wings. Sometimes
you and your friends wanted

to touch the ducks who slept with their heads
buried deep in their feathers. The way

you ran towards them is the way I run
towards this memory: my arms full of

desire, those birds made of air.

The Dead Like Morning

They favor lamps and chandeliers,
the yellow tongues of candles.

Pretty moths, you will find them
in the false light of cities.

Some enjoy the moon with its borrowed
glow, others sit beneath the stars

which appear like holes in a curtain.
Mostly, though, the dead like morning –

sky risen after darkness, shadows
and night fears replaced by color.

They like the chance to pretend
life can begin again, grass

in the fields steaming like coffee.

My Father Watched Westerns

He couldn't get enough of them: those dusty
landscapes on the other side of the screen,
men on horses seeking justice or revenge.
All through my life if he was tired I would

find him in a dark room full of gunfire.
His movie titles included words like *Lone*
and *Lonesome* though mostly families
stuck together and young men learned

to risk their lives for whatever was noble
or right. I could not sit through them;
women were left behind in saloons
with hair and dresses as soft as pillows,

their possibilities perfumed by estrogen.
But it was the men my father was watching.
They had wide hats and leather boots,
masks made of betrayal. My father

remembered the dangerous people
he faced in courtrooms, his arguments
like bullets. His mind was full of places
that were not yet settled, places where

law was new. A man had a horse, a few
friends, some deep internal compass.
People relied on him; what he needed most
was courage. My father related to this.
He knew, afterall, how the west was won.

Places I Have Heard the Ocean

In a cat's throat, in a shell I hold
to my ear – though I'm told
this is the sound of my own
blood. I have heard the ocean
in the city: cars against
the beach of our street. Or in
the subway, waiting for a train
that carries me like a current.
In my bed: place of high and low
tide or in my daughter's skates,
rolling over the sidewalk.
Ocean in the trees when they
fill their heads with wind.
Ocean in the rise and fall:
lungs of everyone I love.

Dunes

The summer I would turn forty we lived in a dune shack named Boris.
Square and wooden it had an outhouse and a clothesline,
a red water pump that pulled at the earth. From our windows
we could see the smoke signals of whales, seals turning
in their blue sheets like babies. There was a frog who lived in
the shade of our bushes and sometimes he buried himself until
only his eyes were visible: two black pebbles watching.
It was cold and rainy and some nights we could not get warm
and some days we were stuck inside our box of wind,
the walls dark with waiting. To keep clean we boiled water
on the stove and stood naked on the porch, pouring.
Our outhouse was a closet of odor with a blue door, a moon
carved in the center; it was the size and shape of a coffin.
I was like the frog, sand pulled around me, while outside
my sister's dog weakened and my grandfather began to shake.
It was as if wind was blowing through the exact center
of my life, hills arranging and rearranging themselves, my shoes
softer and heavier with all that spilled into them. My daughter
brought her sketch books and she bent her head over them
in the lantern light of some other century which was not simpler
just darker and colder like the water we carried to the kitchen
to pour over our dishes, our endless sticky dishes which were dirty
with longing, dirty with the crumbs of what was gone.

What the Wreck Brings

Boxes and crates from other places:
lumber, cotton, pork, hide. Skysail,
Mizzenmast, Four Mast Bark,
Binnacle with a compass still inside.

Dishes

An old boyfriend sent me dishes before
I was married, addressed to me

and not my husband. Each plate
had a fragile, round face; each knife

pointed like a finger. Did I remind
him of dishes? They were heavy

and green and wrapped so they
would not break. Did he mean

that by choosing another man I was
choosing a life as plain as dishes?

Did he want me to think of him
for years, each time I twirled spaghetti

from my plate or spooned happiness
from my bowl? I could see myself

in those dishes the way I can see
myself in a train window: cast over

the passing roads and forests. The dishes
watched me whenever I placed them

on the table or sank them in the sink: as if
he had sent his own hunger, his own eyes.

Gilly

She is made of the farm where she was born:
the hay in the barn, her mother's soft mouth.

She is made of the food from the hand
of the man who wore overalls. She is the couch

and bras she ate as a puppy, the shoes
she stole from my mother. She is the things

she has watched: squirrels,
sticks, birds. She is made of the tears

she has licked, the food we have dropped
under the table. She is made of the nights

when she trots with possums and foxes.
She is shaped by the porch

where she waits for us to come home.

Bowerbirds of New Guinea

The males build circular bowers four feet high
with doorways large enough for a human child.

They weave fruits and flowers and leaves:
each group separated by color. Females choose

their mate based on what he makes. They fly
in groups, cruising this city of huts

and towers, some as simple as a tissue box.
It is a test of strength: a bower assembled

from heavy objects a bird has carried in his beak.
And skill: his ability to weave what he finds

into a home. Many male birds court females
with songs and dances, displays of pretty plumage.

Some offer gifts: snakeskin to line her nest,
sweet fruit. But the Bowerbird builds a house

where he and his lady love will not live. He does it
for sex; he does it so she will have his children.

Or maybe he does it because he must: his mind
full of blueprints, his dreams lit like rooms.

Why I Love a Carousel

It is so old: this desire to ride on the back of an animal
carved before I was born. Give me an ostrich,

a wild pig, a cat with a fish still hanging from its mouth.
Buy a ticket and ride the seasons, birth to death:

rise and fall like a civilization. And the music –
I have never been happier to go nowhere, my hands

around a painted wooden neck. To hear one
in summer across a lawn is to hear your mother

dreaming before she met your father: her face
young and happy, laughter like a sky full of stars.

Shade

My parents let the forest grow wild around their house
so the trees bent protectively over the roof and the ivy
licked the mailbox like flames. They allowed the shade
to grow deep as an ocean: leagues of darkness

leaking down to the lagoon where eels and fish
stirred the water with their tails. When I came to stay
for awhile I was surprised by animals: the white
anger of a possum who hissed at me from the garbage,

the glow of his nocturnal hunger, the strange
nudity of his tail. I was surprised by a spider
in the bathroom as big as my hand: a hairy darkness
that clung to the shower curtain. I scared the turtles

who tucked their bald heads into the shell of their worry,
their fat legs disappearing like rabbits into a
magician's hat. What my parents allowed was
unusual: their neighbors cleared the land, kept

their grass short and poisonous. We let the deer come
to us like secrets, their legs made of silence.
We let the Cottonmouth show us heaven
when she yawned, her long body shining in the sun.

What Night Knows

Night knows the way each animal smells
when it is tired. It knows how the ground
will cool and the grass will weep. Night knows
babies will be born while the sun's eye
is elsewhere; it knows the glow of fear
and the rising tide of sleep. Night can turn
a forest into a tangle of shadows; it can
make a meadow speak. Night is what descends
like a staircase; it is not a coffin though its
walls are wooden and deep. Magic is altered by
its presence: dresses come undone, horses
turn to mice, a shoe may fall and glow.
This is when we practice leaving
our lives: a rehearsal; crickets remember
their violin bows. It is when the witches rise
like birds, that dreary life of sweeping
behind them, each rooftop made of snow.

Spiders

Now that I live in the house where we grew up
I find my brother's trumpet, his chess set,
the newspaper articles my parents

forgot to frame. He does not come back
here though I remember his shape
on the front stairs, his face determined.

We used to sit in a hammock
on the land my father finally sold
and count spiders. There were ten years

between my birth and his. When our
parents lost their money he was home
without the rest of us, the only one

who saw them caught. Now
I am here. I find his track trophies
in my closet because this is where

he learned to run. But I am like the spiders
who still hang over the land we have left:
busy building and rebuilding

what has been knocked down.

Wings

Amelia Earhart was free in her Lockhart Vega
and, all summer, I read about her final journey.
She was following the equator, gravity
beneath her, sky in her eyes. I followed
balloons each time they slipped from
a child's hand. I watched neighborhood
dogs dig under the fence and enter
the danger of the street. Have you seen
the photo of Amelia where she stretches
her arms in front of her plane's wings?
She is happy, you see, demonstrating
how it might be done. Behind her a field
stares up at the white hunger of heaven.
Leaves are free just before they die.
Eleanor Roosevelt asked Amelia to show
her the lights of Washington and they
went up together, still wearing their
evening gowns, their dinner napkins cast aside,
the fine china quiet beneath their flight.

Leaving II

There is something about the way
the light sings in the windows,
the way the children can no longer

keep their faces inside the winter
of their books. Desks are made
of weight and darkness while,

outside, the sky turns the color
of pleasure. When the teacher
descibes fractions he is dividing

the universe into pieces and when
he shows the exact math that
helped man land on the moon

the blackboard hangs before
them like space, all chalky
handwriting as gentle as stars.

The classroom near summer is
a place children are preparing
to leave the way they once left

the darkness of their mothers,
just as they learned to walk out
of the cheerful doors of their nurseries,

their beauty like a new path to the moon.

Shackleton's Decision

At a certain point he decided they could not afford
the dogs. It was someone's job to take them one by one
behind a pile of ice and shoot them. I try to imagine
the arctic night which descended and would not lift,

a darkness that clung to their clothes. Some men objected
because the dogs were warmth and love, reminders
of their previous life where they slept in soft beds,
their bellies warm with supper. Dog tails were made

of joy, their bodies were wrapped in a fur of hope.
I had to put the book down when I read about the dogs
walking willingly into death, following orders,
one clutching an old toy between his teeth. They trusted

the men who led them into this white danger,
this barren cold. My God, they pulled the sleds
full of provisions and barked away the Sea Leopards.
Someone was told to kill the dogs because supplies

were running low and the dogs, gathered around
the fire, their tongues wet with kindness, knew
nothing of betrayal; they knew how to sit and come,
how to please, how to bow their heads, how to stay.

Leaving Kitty Hawk

When I leave the house on Wild Swan Lane our land
will be tangled with hiding, my parents' privacy

so thick it cannot be pierced. The house itself
will be wild: weather and animals inside, cobwebs

over our memories, a snake in the kitchen shedding
its past. It wasn't ever our house though we lived

there while the gauges on the porch measured wind
and predicted difficulty. Here is where my parents

packed our bags for the shore we would occupy
without them. Here is the fireplace that filled

our childhood with smoke. Over there: my mother's
broken bed, her mattress tilted like a planet. When I move

out the story is over, our history on the lawn full of rain.
I will need a boat to reach the next part of my life,

an ocean that carries me as swiftly as tears.

Tourists

Along the beach each family makes a shape:
their umbrellas opening like bright flowers.

They have come to be near the power and sound,
the ocean's wind which blows to us from places

we may never see. In this town most locals
dislike the tourists but I don't mind

the way they wash up here like August jellyfish
or December Conchs. Under that ubiquitous blue

skin: ships, fins, gills. Who can blame
the visitors for hoping to watch a giant ruled

by the moon? Who wouldn't want to touch
the sand and put their feet in the milk of the crash?

Faith Shearin is the author of two previous books of poetry: *The Owl Question* (2002 May Swenson Award) and *The Empty House* (Word Press, 2008). She has received awards from the Barbara Deming Memorial Fund, The Fine Arts Work Center in Provincetown, and the National Endowment for the Arts. Recent work appears in *Ploughshares, Poetry East,* and *North American Review.* Several of her poems have been read aloud by Garrison Keillor on his show *The Writer's Almanac.*

CPSIA information can be obtained at www.ICGtesting.com
Printed in the USA
LVOW13s0710170614

390352LV00006B/15/P

9 781936 205400